DO ONE THING EVERY DAY THAT INSPIRES YOU

A portfolio of creativity by

_____

DATE: __/__/__

Add an epigraph for this book.

_____

_____

_____

_____

_____

_____

_____

_____

_____

_____

"CREATIVITY TAKES COURAGE," according to Henri Matisse. This journal's call to create *every day*, then, may seem daunting. But with quotes to inspire you and original activities to guide you, accepting that challenge will be both exciting and uplifting.

Here you will read the words of men and women in a wide range of creative fields: artists, writers, architects, musicians, dancers, filmmakers, actors, sculptors, chefs, photographers, crafters, and designers of all sorts. You will see how creativity transcends borders and you will be asked to make that leap, too. On special pages sprinkled throughout, you will doodle to themes to spur your creativity and will record personal creative epiphanies throughout the year. You will also be urged to move to the edge or even outside of your creative comfort zone.

Most of the tools you'll need for these challenges will be on hand or easily accessible: pencils, markers, colored pencils, erasers, ink pads, crayons, paint, modeling material, glitter, a camera. More important, though, you will need to engage your own persistence, patience, imagination, and daring as you stretch the boundaries of your creativity.

The entries in this journal are for you to date, so that you can dip in and out as the fancy strikes or as your muse leads you. At the end of the 365 days, you will find that you have built a portfolio of creativity that showcases your most inspired year ever.

I DO NOT SEEK, I FIND.

Pablo Picasso

DATE: __ / __ / __

Randomly find something in your bag or a drawer.
Make a Cubist drawing of it.

Choose an object from nature.
Incorporate it into an abstract sculpture.

DATE: __/__/__

Write a beginning.

_____

_____

_____

_____

_____

_____

DATE: __/__/__

Write an ending.

_____

_____

_____

_____

_____

_____

NOTHING SO DIFFICULT AS A BEGINNING IN POESY, UNLESS PERHAPS THE END.

Lord Byron

I'M INSPIRED BY...
fashion!

DATE: __/__/__

Description:

_____

_____

Designer:

_____

Where I saw it:

_____

DATE: __/__/__

This design inspired me to:

_____

_____

_____

_____

_____

_____

BLOWING IS NOT PLAYING THE FLUTE, YOU MUST MAKE USE OF YOUR FINGERS.

Johann Wolfgang von Goethe

DATE: __ / __ / __

Put ink on your index finger. Create a tune with fingerprint notes.

WE ARE FULL OF RHYTHMS ... OUR PULSE, OUR GESTURES, OUR DIGESTIVE TRACTS, THE LUNAR AND SEASONAL CYCLES.

Yehudi Menuhin

DATE: __/__/__

Put ink on your index finger. Record these body rhythms with hard and soft impressions.

PULSING   BREATHING   BLINKING

DIGESTING   HICCUPING

DESIGN A POSTAGE STAMP.

DATE: __/__/__

DRAW AN ENVELOPE WITH YOUR STAMP ON IT.

TO WRITE IS TO WRITE IS TO WRITE WRITE IS TO WRITE IS TO WRITE.

DATE: __/__/__

The moment you wake up, fill this page with free writing.

random words

an endless sentence

lists

IS TO WRITE IS TO WRITE IS TO

▶ Gertrude Stein

DATE: __/__/__

Just before you go to sleep, fill this page with free writing.

rants

nonsense
words

foreign
words

DATE: __/__/__

Write down a cliché. Rewrite it as a fresh statement.

_____

_____

_____

_____

_____

_____

DATE: __/__/__

Draw a cliché flower. Redraw it unconventionally.

WHAT DISTINGUISHES
A DESIGNER SHEEP
FROM A
DESIGNER GOAT
IS THE ABILITY
TO STROKE A CLICHÉ
UNTIL IT PURRS
LIKE A METAPHOR.

Alan Fletcher

DATE: __/__/__

Go outside and listen. Record a new sound.

CONFORM TO THE RULES, I WISH THERE IS NO THEORY. YOU HAVE

DATE: __ / __ / __

Go inside and listen. Record a new sound.

FILL IN THIS WORD SCALE FOR BEAUTY
FROM "EXQUISITE" TO "GROTESQUE."

EXQUISITE
GROTESQUE

FILL IN THIS WORD SCALE FOR BEHAVIOR
FROM "UNRUFFLED" TO "UNHINGED."

UNRUFFLED
UNHINGED

THE DISCOVERY OF A NEW DISH DOES THAN THE DISCOVERY OF A NEW STAR.

DATE: __/__/__

Write a recipe for an old dish using new ingredients.

MORE FOR HUMAN HAPPINESS

▶ Jean Anthelme Brillat-Savarin

DATE: __/__/__

Write a recipe for an old dessert using new ingredients.

ALWAYS DESIGN A THING BY CONSIDERING
IT IN ITS NEXT LARGER CONTEXT—A CHAIR IN A ROOM,
A ROOM IN A HOUSE, A HOUSE IN AN ENVIRONMENT,
AN ENVIRONMENT IN A CITY PLAN.

Eliel Saarinen

DATE: __/__/__

Design a car around the two wheels below.

DATE: __/__/__

Place your car in a larger context—a parking lot, traffic jam, on an open road, or elsewhere.

I love drawing,
and one
of the things
I wanted to
try was an all-
eraser drawing.

Robert Rauschenberg

DATE: __/__/__

Using a pencil, fill this box with graphite. Then use an eraser to draw an image.

DATE: __/__/__

Return to this drawing later. Use the pencil point to add darker shades and lines to your eraser drawing.

DATE: __ / __ / __

List new pairings of clothes you already own.

_____   _____

_____   _____

_____   _____

_____   _____

_____   _____

_____   _____

_____   _____

_____   _____

_____   _____

_____   _____

DATE: __/__/__

Choose an item of clothing from your closet. Draw it here, adding new clothes—real or imagined—to update it.

A CHOREOGRAPHER IS A POET. I DO NOT CREATE. GOD CREATES. I ASSEMBLE, AND I WILL STEAL FROM EVERYWHERE TO DO IT.

George Balanchine

DATE: __/__/__

Assemble a new dance by combining any of the following. Circle and number the order.

HIP-HOP   TWIST   POLKA   CHARLESTON

WALTZ   ROBOT DISCO   FOX-TROT   JITTERBUG

SQUARE DANCE   MINUET   WORM   RIVER DANCE

CHICKEN DANCE   SWING   BUNNY HOP

DATE: __/__/__

Choose music to accompany your new dance.

_____

_____

_____

_____

_____

_____

DATE: __/__/__

Draw what you see with your eyes closed.

DATE: __/__/__

Describe what you see with your eyes closed.

_____

_____

_____

_____

_____

_____

I SHUT MY EYES IN ORDER TO SEE.

Paul Gauguin

CURVES ARE SO EMOTIONAL.

Piet Mondrian

DATE: __/__/__

Illustrate this idea.

A LINE IS A DOT THAT WENT FOR A WALK.

Paul Klee

DATE: __/__/__

Illustrate this idea.

DATE: _/_/_

0123456789012345678 9

1234567890123

WRITE AN ODE TO A NUMBER.

123456789012345678 90123456789 0123

_____

_____

_____

_____

_____

_____

_____

_____

_____

_____

_____

0123456789012345678 9

DATE: __/__/__

ORANGE BLUE PURPLE RED

CHARTREUSE

SILVER VIOLET GREY

MAUVE BEIGE PINK MINT GOLD BLACK

WRITE AN ODE TO A COLOR.

_____

_____

_____

_____

_____

_____

_____

_____

_____

_____

_____

GREEN YELLOW WHITE ROSE

YOU SEE THINGS;
AND YOU SAY,
"WHY?"
BUT I DREAM
THINGS THAT
NEVER WERE;
AND I SAY,
"WHY NOT?"

George Bernard Shaw

DATE: __/__/__

Name three things you dream of for the future.

_____

_____

_____

_____

_____

_____

DATE: __/__/__

Illustrate one of your dreams for the future.

I'M INSPIRED BY...

a play!

DATE: __/__/__

Title:

_____

Author:

_____

Actors:

_____

_____

_____

_____

Where I saw it:

_____

DATE: __/__/__

This play inspired me to:

_____

_____

_____

_____

HOW CAN YOU WRITE IF YOU CAN'T CRY?

Ring Lardner

DATE: __ / __ / __

When was your last cry? Write the first line of its story.

_____

_____

_____

_____

_____

_____

_____

LET OTHER PENS DWELL ON GUILT AND MISERY.
I QUIT SUCH ODIOUS SUBJECTS AS SOON AS I CAN . . .

Jane Austen

DATE: __/__/__

Write the first line of a story without guilt or misery.

_____

_____

_____

_____

_____

_____

CREATE A CROSS-STITCH PATTERN FOR THIS PILLOW.

DESIGN THIS QUILT BLOCK. USE LIGHT, MEDIUM,
AND DARK SHADES TO CREATE A PATTERN.

DATE: __/__/__

Inspiration after one block:

DATE: __/__/__

Inspiration after two blocks:

IF YOU CAN'T FIND YOUR INSPIRATION BY WALKING AROUND THE BLOCK ONE TIME, GO AROUND TWO BLOCKS—BUT NEVER THREE.

Robert Motherwell

COOKING IS JUST AS CREATIVE AND IMAGINATIVE AN ACTIVITY AS DRAWING, OR WOOD CARVING, OR MUSIC.

Julia Child

DATE: __/__/__

Write and test a recipe that includes four red ingredients.

1 _____   3 _____

2 _____   4 _____

_____

_____

_____

_____

_____

_____

DATE: __/__/__

Buy an ingredient you have never used before.
Create a dish showcasing it.

_____
_____
_____
_____
_____
_____
_____
_____
_____
_____
_____
_____
_____

THE MUSES LOVE THE MORNING.

Thomas Fuller

DATE: __/__/__

Listen to your morning muse and record below.
Inspiration at ___ a.m.:

_____

_____

_____

_____

_____

_____

DATE: __/__/__

Listen to your morning muse and record below.
Inspiration at ___ a.m.:

_____

_____

_____

_____

_____

_____

DATE: __/__/__

SET A TIMER FOR TWO MINUTES.
LIST ALL THE USES YOU CAN THINK OF FOR A PAPER CLIP.

DATE: __/__/__

SET A TIMER FOR TWO MINUTES.

LIST ALL THE USES YOU CAN THINK OF FOR A SPOON.

_____

_____

_____

_____

_____

_____

_____

_____

_____

_____

_____

_____

_____

_____

_____

BETTER TO GIVE THE GESTURE THAN THE OUTLINE OF THE ARM.

Robert Henri

DATE: __/__/__

Draw arm gestures to express:

CONVICTION

ANGER

FRIGHT

AWE

APPROVAL

Fill in these faces to express:

SHOCK

DISAPPOINTMENT

CURIOSITY

SHAME

JOY

doo

Doodle the ocean.

Doodle the sky.

ADD AN ARROW MADE UP OF WORDS TO THIS CONCRETE POEM.

Guillaume Apollinaire

WRITE A FOUND POEM.

Find a line
from a newspaper,
speech,
set of instructions,
or ad.
Break it into phrases
to create a poem.

_____

_____

_____

_____

_____

_____

_____

_____

_____

_____

DATE: __/__/__

Draw a piece of furniture from the top.

DATE: __/__/__

Draw the same piece of furniture from the side.

WHAT A DELIGHTFUL THING THIS PERSPECTIVE IS!

Paolo Uccello

NO HANDYCRAFT CAN WITH OUR ART COMPARE, FOR POTS ARE MADE OF WHAT WE POTTERS ARE.

▲

Potters' motto from the eighteenth century

▼

DATE: __ / __ / __

Make something out of modeling material that demonstrates who you are. Place a photograph of it here.

Create an inspiration board—a collage of magazine cutouts, photographs, fabrics, doodles, and anything else that fires your creativity.

Take a photograph and place it here.

DATE: __ / __ / __

List the characters you would be most interested to play.

_____

_____

_____

_____

_____

_____

_____

_____

_____

_____

_____

DATE: __/__/__

Cast *Gone with the Wind* with contemporary actors and actresses.

Scarlett:

_____

Rhett:

_____

Ashley:

_____

Melanie:

_____

Mammy:

_____

Rightly thought of there is poetry in peaches, even when they are canned.

Harley Granville-Barker

DATE: __/__/__

Write a poem about canned peaches.

_____

_____

_____

_____

_____

_____

DATE: __/__/__

Draw the can in the style of Andy Warhol.

AT PAINFUL TIMES, WHEN COMPOSITION IS IMPOSSIBLE
AND READING NOT ENOUGH, GRAMMARS
AND DICTIONARIES ARE EXCELLENT FOR DISTRACTION.

▲
Elizabeth Barrett Browning
▼

DATE: __ / __ / __

Books that distract you:

_____

_____

_____

_____

_____

_____

Books that inspire you:

DON'T WORRY ABOUT MISTAKES. MAKING THINGS OUT OF MISTAKES, THAT'S CREATIVITY.

Peter Max

Turn this accidental ink splat into a picture of a cow.

Make a sign around this mistakenly backward letter.

DESIGN A MONUMENT TO YOUR FAVORITE AUTHOR.

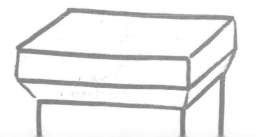

DESIGN A MONUMENT TO YOUR FAVORITE MUSICIAN.

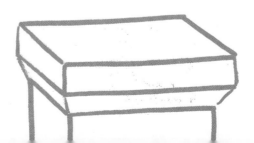

I'M INSPIRED BY...

food!

DATE: __/__/__

Dish:

_____

Ingredients:

_____

_____

_____

_____

Where I tasted it:

_____

DATE: __/__/__

What I was inspired to cook:

_____

_____

_____

_____

_____

_____

LESS IS MORE.

Ludwig Mies van der Rohe

DATE: __/__/__

Draw an elaborate building.

DATE: __/__/__

Redraw the building, removing three elements.

DATE: __/__/__

CHART A TEXTILE PATTERN.

DRAW THE PATTERN ONTO A SHIRT.

DATE: __/__/__

Write a novel in six words.

     _____

     _____

     _____

     _____

     _____

     _____

DATE: __/__/__

Write a memoir in six words.

     _____

     _____

     _____

     _____

     _____

     _____

FOR SALE: BABY SHOES, NEVER WORN.

Ernest Hemingway, attrib.

Biting my truant pen, beating myself for spite: "Fool," said my Muse to me, "look in thy heart, and write."

Sir Philip Sidney

DATE: __/__/__

Describe a heartfelt moment.

_____

_____

_____

_____

_____

_____

DATE: __/__/__

Draw a heartfelt moment.

TO SING IS AN EXPRESSION OF YOUR BEING, A BEING WHICH IS BECOMING.

Maria Callas

DATE: __/__/__

List the songs that best express your being.

_____

_____

_____

_____

_____

_____

I MERELY TOOK THE ENERGY
IT TAKES TO POUT AND WROTE SOME BLUES.

Duke Ellington

DATE: __/__/__

List the music that best expresses your lows and highs.

_____

_____

_____

_____

_____

_____

TRANSFORM SNEAKERS, A T-SHIRT, OR A BAG USING STUDS, SPIKES, GLITTER, BUTTONS, EMBROIDERY THREAD, PAINT, OR ANYTHING ELSE THAT WILL MAKE IT A FASHION STATEMENT.

Place a photograph here.

DECORATE THIS CAKE FOR A SPECIFIC OCCASION.

A DREAM THAT IS NOT INTERPRETED
IS LIKE A LETTER THAT IS UNREAD.

Talmud

DATE: __/__/__

Interpret a dream you had.

_____

_____

_____

_____

_____

_____

_____

_____

_____

_____

I DREAM A LOT.
I DO MORE PAINTING WHEN I'M NOT PAINTING.
IT'S IN THE SUBCONSCIOUS.

Andrew Wyeth

DATE: __/__/__

Sketch a painting in your subconscious.

Doodle a pet.

Doodle a wild beast.

FASHION IS ARCHITECTURE: IT IS A MATTER OF PROPORTIONS.

Coco Chanel

DATE: __/__/__

Draw a dress with
excellent proportions.

Draw a suit with excellent proportions.

REPURPOSE A KITCHEN UTENSIL FOR YOUR OFFICE.

Utensil:

_____

New use:

DATE: __/__/__

REPURPOSE AN OFFICE UTENSIL FOR YOUR KITCHEN.

Utensil:

_____

New use:

DATE: __ / __ / __

What favorite author would you call? What would you ask or say?

_____

_____

_____

_____

_____

_____

DATE: __ / __ / __

What favorite artist would you call? What would you ask or say?

_____

_____

_____

_____

_____

_____

WHAT REALLY KNOCKS ME
OUT IS A BOOK THAT, WHEN
YOU'RE ALL DONE READING
IT, YOU WISH
THE AUTHOR THAT
WROTE IT WAS A TERRIFIC
FRIEND OF YOURS AND
YOU COULD CALL HIM UP
ON THE PHONE WHENEVER
YOU FELT LIKE IT.

J. D. Salinger

A MASTER NEEDS QUIET. CALM AND QUIET ARE HIS MOST IMPERATIVE NEEDS.

Richard Wagner

DATE: __/__/__

What aspects of your creativity need calm and quiet?

_____

_____

_____

_____

_____

_____

DATE: __/__/__

What you created in calm and quiet:

_____

_____

_____

_____

_____

_____

I DON'T SEEK THE TITLE OF "INOFFENSIVE,"
WHICH I THINK IS ONE OF THE NASTIEST THINGS THAT
COULD BE SAID ABOUT AN INDIVIDUAL WRITER.

Christopher Hitchens

DATE: __/__/__

Fill in this scale with names of writers, ranked from "inoffensive"
to "offensive."

INOFFENSIVE
OFFENSIVE

MANY WEARING RAPIERS ARE AFRAID OF GOOSE QUILLS.

William Shakespeare

DATE: __/__/__

Use your goose quill to vent about a public official or a professional enemy.

_____

_____

_____

_____

_____

_____

DATE: __ / __ / __

HOLD THE BASE OF A WINE GLASS SECURELY ON THE TABLE.
RUN YOUR WET FINGER ROUND AND ROUND THE RIM.
DESCRIBE THE SOUNDS YOU HEAR.

The sound of an animal:

_____

The sound of nature:

_____

The sound of someone you know:

_____

The sound of an emotion:

_____

The sound of something else:

_____

DATE: __/__/__

USE A PENCIL TO TAP A SERIES OF GLASSES FILLED WITH DIFFERENT LEVELS OF WATER. LIST THE TUNES YOU CAN PLAY.

_____

_____

_____

_____

_____

_____

_____

_____

_____

_____

_____

_____

IF BOTTICELLI WERE ALIVE TODAY, HE'D BE WORKING FOR *VOGUE.*

Peter Ustinov

DATE: __/__/__

Design a *Vogue* cover with Botticelli as the art director.

Use Botticelli's Venus
to model swimwear.

I'M INSPIRED BY...
a garden!

DATE: __/__/__

Name:

_____

Location:

_____

Season:

_____

Flowers:

_____

_____

DATE: __/__/__

I was inspired by this garden to:

_____

_____

_____

_____

_____

_____

IT IS BY SITTING DOWN TO WRITE EVERY MORNING THAT ONE BECOMES A WRITER.

Gerald Brenan

DATE: __/__/__

This morning's writing:

_____

_____

_____

_____

_____

_____

DO NOT FAIL, AS YOU GO ON, TO DRAW SOMETHING EVERY DAY.

Cennino Cennini

DATE: __/__/__

Today's drawing:

CREATE A TITLE FOR A HORROR MOVIE.

DESIGN THE POSTER FOR YOUR HORROR MOVIE.

DATE: __/__/__

Artists I love:

_____

_____

_____

_____

_____

_____

DATE: __/__/__

Musicians I love:

_____

_____

_____

_____

_____

_____

If you fall in love
with Van Gogh or Matisse
or John Oliver Killens, or
if you fall in love
with the music of Coltrane,
the music of Aretha
Franklin, or the music
of Chopin—find some
beautiful art and admire it,
and realize that
that was created by
human beings just like you,
no more human, no less.

Maya Angelou

LOVE IS A CANVAS FURNISHED BY NATURE AND EMBROIDERED BY IMAGINATION.

Voltaire

DATE: __/__/__

Design a romantic garden.

Design an embroidery pattern that shows your love.

KISSING DON'T LAST; COOKERY DO!

George Meredith

DATE: __/__/__

Describe a kiss that was fleeting.

_____

_____

_____

_____

_____

_____

DATE: __/__/__

Describe a dish that is immortal.

_____

_____

_____

_____

_____

_____

DATE: __/__/__

Draw the moon as an astronaut might see it.

DATE: __/__/__

Draw the moon as an Impressionist painter might see it.

THE MOON IS A DIFFERENT THING TO EACH ONE OF US.

Frank Borman

DRAW A STICK FIGURE USING ONLY CIRCLES.

DRAW THE SUN USING ONLY LINES.

A NOVEL IS A MIRROR CARRIED ALONG A MAIN ROAD.

Stendhal

DATE: __ / __ / __

Walk down a main road. Record your reflections.

_____

_____

_____

_____

_____

_____

I REALLY BELIEVE THERE ARE THINGS NOBODY WOULD SEE IF I DIDN'T PHOTOGRAPH THEM.

Diane Arbus

DATE: __/__/__

Place a photograph here of something seen only by you.

Doodle happiness.

Doodle sadness.

FIND A SET OF STARS IN THE NIGHT SKY TO MAKE A NEW CONSTELLATION. DRAW THE STARS AND THE FIGURE AROUND IT.

DATE: __/__/__

NAME YOUR CONSTELLATION AND WRITE ITS MYTH.

_____

_____

_____

_____

_____

_____

_____

_____

_____

_____

_____

_____

_____

_____

_____

_____

_____

_____

THE PHYSICIAN CAN BURY HIS MISTAKES, BUT THE ARCHITECT CAN ONLY ADVISE HIS CLIENT TO PLANT VINES.

Frank Lloyd Wright

DATE: __/__/__

How can you bury this mistake?

I CAN'T WRITE FIVE WORDS BUT THAT I CHANGE SEVEN.

Dorothy Parker

DATE: __ / __ / __

Write the first two lines of a story. Then rewrite them.

_____

_____

_____

_____

_____

_____

I wrote _____ words. I changed _____ words.

IT IS ALL VERY WELL TO BE ABLE TO WRITE BOOKS, BUT CAN YOU WAGGLE YOUR EARS?

James Matthew Barrie

DATE: __/__/__

What I can do with my face (check off):

[ ] waggle my ears

[ ] raise one eyebrow

[ ] roll my tongue

[ ] lick my elbow

[ ] touch my tongue to my nose

[ ] cross my eyes

[ ] flare my nostrils

[ ] make a fish face

[ ] other: _____

_____

TO ME, THE BODY SAYS WHAT WORDS CANNOT.

Martha Graham

DATE: __/__/__

Express what words cannot using this torso.

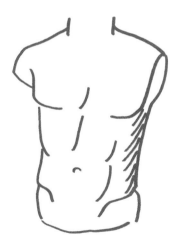

STYLE HER HAIRDO.

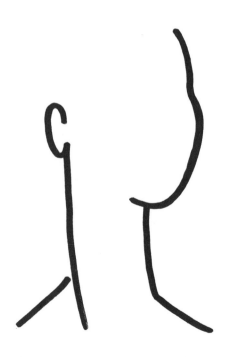

STYLE HIS HAIRDO.

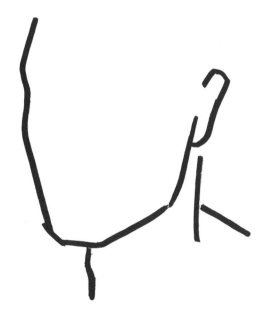

A WOMAN MUST HAVE MONEY AND A ROOM OF HER OWN IF SHE IS TO WRITE FICTION.

Virginia Woolf

DATE: __ / __ / __

Describe or draw your ideal writing room.

THE TOOLS I NEED FOR MY WORK ARE PAPER, TOBACCO, FOOD, AND A LITTLE WHISKEY.

William Faulkner

DATE: __/__/__

List the tools you need for your creative work.

_____

_____

_____

_____

_____

_____

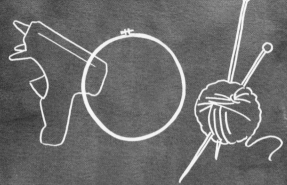

I'M INSPIRED BY...
a craft!

DATE: __/__/__

Craft:

_____

Artist:

_____

Medium:

_____

Where I saw it:

_____

DATE: __/__/__

This craft inspired me to:

_____

_____

_____

_____

_____

_____

I SAW AN ANGEL IN THE BLOCK OF MARBLE AND I JUST CHISELED 'TIL I SET HIM FREE.

Michelangelo

DATE: __/__/__

Shade the areas you would chisel away to set a sculpture free.

ENGRAVING, THEN, IS, IN BRIEF TERMS, THE ART OF THE SCRATCH.

John Ruskin

DATE: __/__/__

Using a wax crayon, color this entire page. Scratch in your drawing with a pin.

DESIGN A TATTOO FOR YOUR BACK.

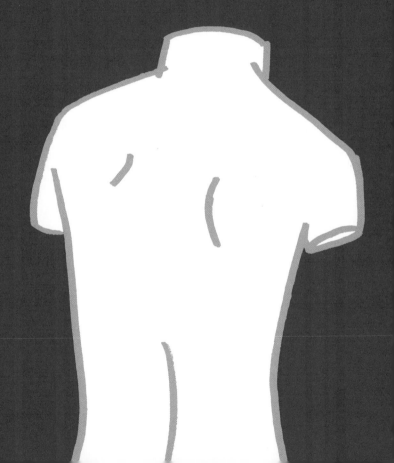

DESIGN A TATTOO FOR YOUR ARM.

RECOGNIZING THE NEED IS
THE PRIMARY CONDITION FOR DESIGN.

Charles Eames

DATE: __ / __ / __

Create a useful object.

ALL ART IS QUITE USELESS.

Oscar Wilde

DATE: __/__/__

Create a useless object.

IN A PORTRAIT, I'M LOOKING FOR THE SILENCE IN SOMEBODY.

Henri Cartier-Bresson

DATE: __/__/__

Place a picture here showing the silence in somebody else.

DATE: __/__/__

Place a selfie here showing the silence in you.

GIVE ME A LAUNDRY LIST AND I'LL SET IT TO MUSIC.

Gioacchino Rossini

DATE: __/__/__

Write your shopping list or to-do list here.

_____

_____

_____

_____

_____

_____

Choose a melody to set it to.

_____

_____

_____

Sing.

TO INVENT, YOU NEED A GOOD IMAGINATION AND A PILE OF JUNK.

▲

Thomas Alva Edison

▼

DATE: __/__/__

Create a found-art sculpture from "junk."

Place a photograph here.

CREATE A NEW CEREAL AND DESIGN ITS BOX.

DATE: __/__/__

CREATE A NEW KIND OF PACKAGING FOR YOUR CEREAL.

DATE: __/__/__

Describe a time when you stood up to live.

_____

_____

_____

_____

_____

_____

DATE: __/__/__

Draw a scene when you stood up to live.

HOW VAIN IT IS TO SIT DOWN TO WRITE WHEN YOU HAVE NOT STOOD UP TO LIVE!

Henry David Thoreau

Doodle a waltz.

Doodle hip-hop.

EVERY MAN IS A POET WHEN HE IS IN LOVE.

Plato

DATE: __/__/__

Create a valentine.

EVERY LEAF SPEAKS BLISS TO ME, FLUTTERING FROM THE AUTUMN TREE.

Emily Brontë

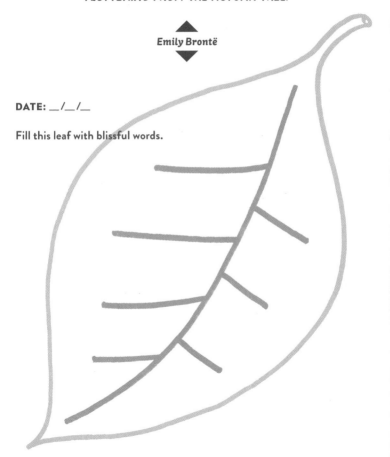

DATE: __/__/__

Fill this leaf with blissful words.

DATE: __ / __ / __

Pick a spot. Sketch it at 9 a.m.

Return to the same spot. Sketch it at 9 p.m.

Looking back, I imagine I was always writing. Twaddle it was, too. But better far write twaddle or anything, anything, than nothing at all.

Katherine Mansfield

Write twaddle.

_____

_____

_____

_____

_____

_____

Draw twaddle.

PERIODS OF TRANQUILITY ARE SELDOM PROLIFIC OF CREATIVE ACHIEVEMENT. MANKIND HAS TO BE STIRRED UP.

Alfred North Whitehead

DATE: __/__/__

What stirs up your creativity:

_____

_____

_____

_____

_____

_____

DATE: __/__/__

What you created when you were stirred up:

_____

_____

_____

_____

_____

_____

GOD LOVETH ADVERBS.

Bishop Joseph Hall

DATE: __/__/__

Add adverbs to this passage so that God will love it.

Noah called his family and hustled them and all the animals onto the ark. He was worried about the graying skies and the storm that was approaching. The dogs barked, the lions roared, and the children whined and raced around until he had to rebuke them all.

Which version do you prefer?

I BELIEVE THE ROAD TO HELL IS PAVED WITH ADVERBS, AND I WILL SHOUT IT FROM THE ROOFTOPS.

Stephen King

DATE: __/__/__

Restore these altered sentences from *Carrie* to the way King intended.

Carrie very slowly turned off the shower. It died finally in a drip and a gurgle. It wasn't until she tentatively stepped out that they all suddenly saw the blood running rapidly down her leg.

Which version do you prefer?

CREATE A COMIC STRIP OF A PERSONAL EXPERIENCE.
DRAW ILLUSTRATIONS IN THESE FOUR BOXES.

ADD SPEECH BUBBLES.

YOU CAN ONLY WRITE ABOUT WHAT BITES YOU.

Tom Stoppard

DATE: _/_/_

Write four lines of biting dialogue.

EVERY TIME I PAINT A PORTRAIT I LOSE A FRIEND.

John Singer Sargent

DATE: __ / __ / __

Paint an unflattering portrait of a friend.

I'M INSPIRED BY... a piece of music!

DATE: __/__/__

Title:

_____

Composer:

_____

Performers:

_____

_____

_____

Where I heard it:

_____

DATE: __/__/__

This music inspired me to:

_____

_____

_____

DATE: __/__/__

Write a poem about your best moment.

_____

_____

_____

_____

_____

_____

DATE: __/__/__

Write a poem about your happiest moment.

_____

_____

_____

_____

_____

_____

POETRY IS THE RECORD OF THE BEST AND HAPPIEST MOMENTS OF THE HAPPIEST AND BEST MINDS.

Percy Bysshe Shelley

DRAW A FLOWER WITH YOUR LEFT HAND.

DRAW A FLOWER WITH YOUR RIGHT HAND.

SOUP OF THE EVENING, BEAUTIFUL SOUP!

Lewis Carroll

DATE: __/__/__

Create a beautiful soup from ingredients in your kitchen. List them here.

_____

_____

_____

_____

_____

_____

_____

_____

_____

_____

I WAS THIRTY-TWO WHEN I STARTED COOKING: UP UNTIL THEN, I JUST ATE.

Julia Child

DATE: __ / __ / __

Name a food you used to just eat.

_____

_____

Describe how you now cook with it.

_____

_____

_____

_____

_____

_____

THERE ARE PAINTERS WHO TRANSFORM THE SUN
TO A YELLOW SPOT, BUT THERE ARE OTHERS
WHO WITH THE HELP OF THEIR ART AND THEIR INTELLIGENCE,
TRANSFORM A YELLOW SPOT INTO THE SUN.

Pablo Picasso

DATE: __ / __ / __

Color this spot and transform it.

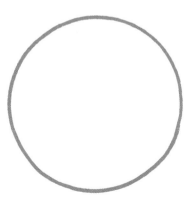

WITH COLOR ONE OBTAINS AN ENERGY THAT SEEMS TO STEM FROM WITCHCRAFT.

Henri Matisse

DATE: __/__/__

Fill these in with the most bewitching colors.

A PASSION FOR THE DRAMATIC ART
IS INHERENT IN THE NATURE OF MAN.

Edwin Forrest

DATE: __/__/__

Display your dramatic nature as you (check off):

[ ] brush your teeth

[ ] make an entrance

[ ] make a departure

[ ] tell a tale

[ ] eat a meal

[ ] other: _____

_____

PRETENDING IS NOT JUST PLAY.
PRETENDING IS IMAGINED POSSIBILITY.

Meryl Streep

DATE: __/__/__

Today I pretended:

_____

_____

_____

_____

_____

What resulted:

_____

_____

_____

_____

_____

ART WILL MAKE OUR STREETS AS BEAUTIFUL AS THE WOODS, AS ELEVATING AS THE MOUNTAINSIDE.

William Morris

DATE: __/__/__

Draw a bench, fountain, lamp, or other urban furniture that would make your street more beautiful.

DATE: __/__/__

Draw landscaping that would make your street more beautiful.

DRAW A SCENE IN PERSPECTIVE,
WHERE THE CLOSER OBJECTS ARE LARGER.

DRAW THE SCENE IN REVERSE PERSPECTIVE,
WHERE THE CLOSER OBJECTS ARE SMALLER.

THE GREATEST PART OF A WRITER'S TIME IS SPENT IN READING, IN ORDER TO WRITE; A MAN WILL TURN OVER HALF A LIBRARY TO MAKE ONE BOOK.

Samuel Johnson

DATE: __ / __ / __

List the books you would read to prepare for writing.

_____

_____

_____

_____

_____

_____

_____

SOME BOOKS ARE TO BE TASTED, OTHERS TO BE SWALLOWED, AND SOME FEW TO BE CHEWED AND DIGESTED.

Sir Francis Bacon

DATE: __ / __ / __

Books to taste:

_____

_____

Books to swallow:

_____

_____

Books to digest:

_____

_____

Doodle flying.

Doodle swimming.

WRITE SOME IDEAS FOR A NEW TV TALENT SHOW
AND GIVE IT A NAME.

COMPOSE A PANEL OF JUDGES FOR YOUR NEW TV TALENT SHOW.

1 _____

2 _____

3 _____

4 _____

5 _____

DRAW A HOUSE WITHOUT LIFTING YOUR PENCIL.

DRAW A BRIDGE WITHOUT LIFTING YOUR PENCIL.

"**What is the use of a book,**" **thought Alice,** "**without pictures or conversation?**"

Lewis Carroll

DATE: __/__/__

Open a book at random, read a page, and illustrate it.

Title: _____ Page: _____

DATE: __/__/__

Open a book at random, read a page, and insert a conversation.

Title: _____ Page: _____

Conversation:

_____

_____

_____

_____

PHOTOGRAPH A COMMON OBJECT FROM AN UNCOMMON ANGLE.

Place it here.

PHOTOGRAPH AN ORDINARY PERSON FROM
AN EXTRAORDINARY ANGLE.

Place it here.

I LIKE AN EMPTY WALL BECAUSE I CAN IMAGINE WHAT I LIKE ON IT.

Georgia O'Keeffe

DATE: __/__/__

Draw what you like on these walls.

IT IS COMPARATIVELY EASY TO ACHIEVE A CERTAIN UNITY
IN A PICTURE BY ALLOWING ONE COLOR TO DOMINATE, OR BY
MUTING ALL THE COLORS. MATISSE DID NEITHER.
HE CLASHED HIS COLORS TOGETHER LIKE CYMBALS AND
THE EFFECT WAS LIKE A LULLABY.

John Berger

DATE: __/__/__

Clash colors together on this page.

I'M INSPIRED BY . . .

a film!

DATE: __/__/__

Title:

_____

Director:

_____

Actors:

_____

_____

_____

_____

Where I saw it:

_____

DATE: __/__/__

This film inspired me to:

_____

_____

DATE: __/__/__

Set the time and day to begin your novel.

 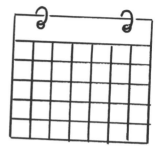

DATE: __/__/__

Start writing here.

_____

_____

_____

_____

_____

_____

AMONG THE MANY PROBLEMS THAT BESET THE NOVELIST, NOT THE LEAST WEIGHTY IS THE CHOICE OF THE MOMENT AT WHICH TO BEGIN HIS NOVEL.

Vita Sackville-West

CHANGE YOUR TRAVEL ROUTE FOR ONE DAY.
MAP IT HERE.

WHAT WAS DIFFERENT?

_____

_____

_____

DATE: __/__/__

CHANGE THE ORDER OF YOUR MEALS FOR ONE DAY.
RECORD THEM HERE.

- MENU -

Meal 1
_____
_____

Meal 2
_____
_____

Meal 3
_____
_____

WHAT WAS DIFFERENT?

_____
_____
_____

BIOGRAPHIES ARE BUT THE CLOTHES AND
OF THE MAN HIMSELF CANNOT BE

DATE: __/__/__

Create a biography of this
woman by dressing her.

BUTTONS OF THE MAN. THE BIOGRAPHY WRITTEN. ▶ Mark Twain

DATE: _/_/_

Create a biography of this
man by dressing him.

HEARD MELODIES ARE SWEET, BUT THOSE UNHEARD ARE SWEETER; THEREFORE, YE SOFT PIPES, PLAY ON.

John Keats

DATE: __/__/__

Describe the melody you hear from this Grecian urn.

_____

_____

_____

_____

_____

_____

_____

_____

ARCHITECTURE IN GENERAL IS FROZEN MUSIC.

Friedrich Wilhelm Joseph von Schelling

DATE: __/__/__

Match a building to a piece of music.

&

VISION IS THE ART OF SEEING THINGS INVISIBLE.

Jonathan Swift

DATE: __/__/__

Draw your vision of friendship.

DATE: __/__/__

Draw your vision of love.

DATE: __/__/__

AS AN AUTHOR

AS AN ARCHITECT

AS AN ACTOR

SIGNATURE...

DATE: __/__/__

AS AN ARTIST

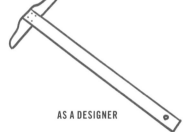

AS A DESIGNER

AS A MUSICIAN

Doodle sunrise.

Doodle sunset.

SOME PEOPLE WILL TELL YOU THAT THERE IS A GREAT DEAL OF POETRY AND FINE SENTIMENT IN A CHEST OF TEA.

Ralph Waldo Emerson

DATE: __/__/__

Drink a cup of tea and describe your sentiments.

_____

_____

_____

_____

_____

_____

DATE: __/__/__

Attach dry tea leaves here and transform them into art.

DESIGN A STORE WINDOW WITH A HALLOWEEN THEME.

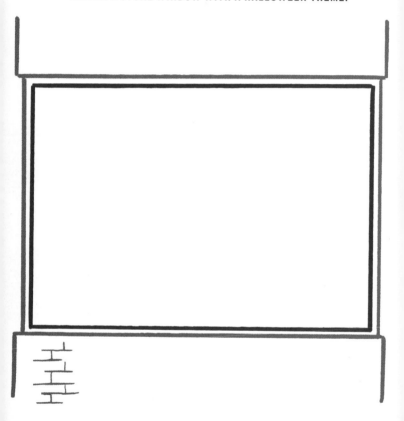

DESIGN A STORE WINDOW WITH A VALENTINE'S DAY THEME.

THE SECRET OF ALL
IS TO WRITE IN THE GUSH,
THE THROB, THE FLOOD,
OF THE MOMENT—
TO PUT THINGS DOWN
WITHOUT DELIBERATION—
WITHOUT WORRYING
ABOUT THEIR STYLE—
WITHOUT WAITING FOR A
FIT TIME OR PLACE.

Walt Whitman

DATE: __/__/__

Write without deliberation.

_____

_____

_____

_____

_____

_____

DATE: __/__/__

Draw without deliberation.

THE POET IS A REPORTER INTERVIEWING HIS OWN HEART.

Christopher Morley

DATE: __/__/__

Interview your heart about a person: who, what, where, when, and why?

_____

_____

_____

_____

_____

_____

DATE: __/__/__

Interview your heart about a place: who, what, where, when, and why?

_____

_____

_____

_____

_____

_____

DATE: __/__/__

Mark off the days until you reach a brilliant idea.

DATE: __/__/__

Brilliant idea:

It takes a lot
of time to be a
genius, you have
to sit around
so much doing
nothing, really
doing nothing.

Gertrude Stein

DRAW THE BACKS OF THE PRESIDENTS' HEADS
ON MOUNT RUSHMORE.

DRAW THE MONA LISA STANDING UP.

DATE: __/__/__

I am bored by:

_____

_____

_____

_____

_____

_____

DATE: __/__/__

I avoided boredom by creating:

_____

_____

_____

_____

_____

_____

THE LIFE OF
THE CREATIVE MAN
IS LED, DIRECTED,
AND CONTROLLED
BY BOREDOM.
AVOIDING BOREDOM
IS ONE OF OUR MOST
IMPORTANT PURPOSES.

Saul Steinberg

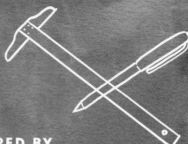

I'M INSPIRED BY...

a design!

DATE: __/__/__

Design:

_____

_____

Artist:

_____

Material:

_____

_____

Where I saw it:

_____

DATE: __/__/__

This design inspired me to:

_____

_____

_____

EVERY MAN'S WORK, WHETHER IT BE LITERATURE OR MUSIC OR PICTURES OR ARCHITECTURE OR ANYTHING ELSE, IS ALWAYS A PORTRAIT OF HIMSELF.

Samuel Butler

DATE: __ / __ / __

Draw yourself as a building.

DATE: __ / __ / __

Write yourself as music.

DATE: __ / __ / __

DESIGN A LOGO OF YOUR INITIALS.

DECORATE A TOTE BAG WITH YOUR LOGO.

DATE: __ / __ / __

My hunch:

_____

Its message:

_____

My creation:

DATE: __/__/__

My hunch:

_____

Its message:

_____

My creation:

I HAVE NOTHING TO SAY AND I AM SAYING IT
AND THAT IS POETRY AS I NEEDED IT.

John Cage

DATE: __ / __ / __

Write a poem that says nothing.

_____

_____

_____

_____

_____

_____

_____

. . . A SHOW ABOUT NOTHING.

Jerry Seinfeld

DATE: __/__/__

Write a joke about nothing.

_____

_____

_____

_____

_____

_____

_____

I DON'T DESIGN CLOTHES. I DESIGN DREAMS.

Ralph Lauren

DATE: __/__/__

Dream a setting.

DATE: __/__/__

Design an outfit to wear in your
dreamy setting.

WRITE DOWN FOUR LINES OF AN OVERHEARD
PHONE CONVERSATION. FILL IN THE WORDS OF THE SECOND
SPEAKER TO CREATE A ROMANTIC DIALOGUE.

Words heard: _____

Words imagined: _____

Words heard: _____

Words imagined: _____

Words heard: _____

Words imagined: _____

Words heard: _____

Words imagined: _____

WRITE DOWN FOUR LINES OF AN OVERHEARD
PHONE CONVERSATION. FILL IN THE WORDS OF THE SECOND
SPEAKER TO CREATE A SINISTER PLOT.

Words heard: _____

Words imagined: _____

Words heard: _____

Words imagined: _____

Words heard: _____

Words imagined: _____

Words heard: _____

Words imagined: _____

TELL ME WHAT YOU EAT,
AND I WILL TELL YOU WHAT YOU ARE.

Jean Anthelme Brillat-Savarin

DATE: __/__/__

Turn your favorite food into a self-portrait.

Place a photograph here.

GOOD PAINTING IS LIKE GOOD COOKING;
IT CAN BE TRUSTED, BUT NOT EXPLAINED.

Maurice de Vlaminck

DATE: __/__/__

Favorite painting:

Favorite dish:

DANCING IS THE POETRY OF THE FOOT.

John Dryden

DATE: __/__/__

Finish these lines of feet moving in iambic pentameter, then dance them.

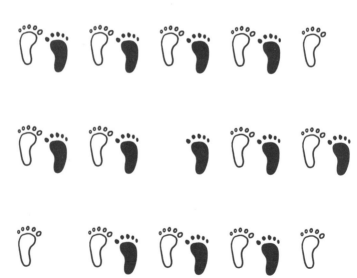

ALWAYS THE QUESTION FOR DANCERS IS: CAN WE FLY?

Jean-Christophe Maillot

DATE: __/__/__

Draw yourself leaping your highest.

Doodle winter.

Doodle summer.

TRUE CREATIVITY IS CHARACTERIZED DEPENDENT ON THE ONE BEFORE AND

DATE: __/__/__

Fill in the missing first frames.

DATE: __/__/__

Fill in the missing last frames.

COVER THIS WINDOW WITH CURTAINS.

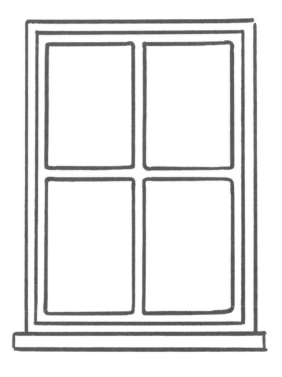

UPHOLSTER THIS WING CHAIR WITH FABRIC.

TO ONE IT IS A MIGHTY HEAVENLY GODDESS, TO THE OTHER AN EXCELLENT COW THAT FURNISHES HIM WITH BUTTER.

Friedrich von Schiller

DATE: __/__/__

List things you consider heavenly that others might think mundane.

_____

_____

_____

_____

_____

_____

A FOOL SEES NOT THE SAME TREE THAT A WISE MAN SEES.

William Blake

DATE: __/__/__

Draw two trees—the fool's and the wise man's.

THE STRUCTURE OF A PLAY IS ALWAYS HOME TO ROOST. ▶ Arthur Miller

DATE: __/__/__

Write a play synopsis in one sentence.

_____

_____

_____

_____

_____

_____

THE STORY OF HOW THE BIRDS CAME

DATE: __/__/__

Draw the set for the first act of your play.

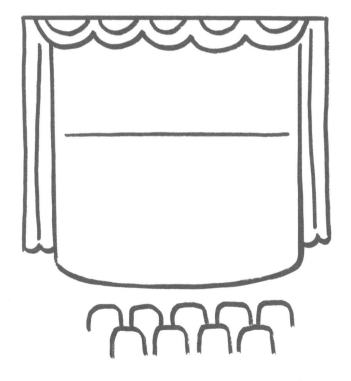

TO SEE A WORLD IN A GRAIN OF SAND
AND HEAVEN IN A WILD FLOWER,
HOLD INFINITY IN THE PALM OF YOUR HAND
AND ETERNITY IN AN HOUR.

William Blake

DATE: __/__/__

Illustrate this idea.

THERE IS MATERIAL ENOUGH IN A SINGLE FLOWER FOR THE ORNAMENT OF A SCORE OF CATHEDRALS.

John Ruskin

DATE: __/__/__

Observe a flower. Use its elements to design a cathedral.

GIVE THIS HAND A MANICURE FOR A NIGHT ON THE TOWN.

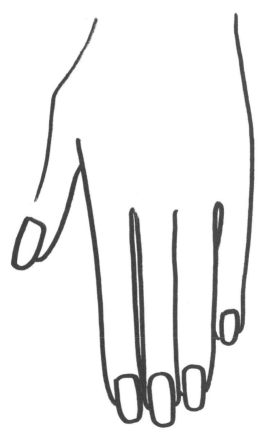

GIVE THIS FOOT A PEDICURE FOR A BAREFOOT BEACH PARTY.

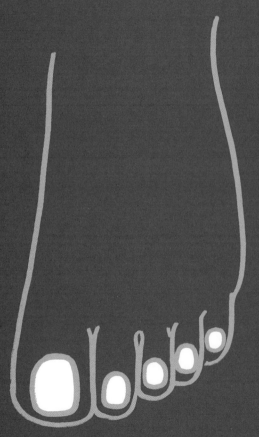

IT DOES NOT NEED THAT A POEM SHOULD BE LONG.
EVERY WORD WAS ONCE A POEM.

▲
Ralph Waldo Emerson
▼

DATE: __ / __ / __

Fill this page with single-word poems.

_____   _____

_____   _____

_____   _____

_____   _____

_____   _____

_____   _____

_____   _____

_____   _____

_____   _____

THIS THE JUST RIGHT OF POETS EVER WAS, AND WILL BE STILL, TO COIN WHAT WORDS THEY PLEASE.

John Oldham

DATE: __/__/__

Coin a word:

_____

Define it:

_____

_____

_____

I'M INSPIRED BY...

a building!

DATE: __/__/__

Name:

_____

Materials:

_____

_____

Architect:

_____

Location:

_____

DATE: __/__/__

This building inspired me to:

_____

_____

_____

_____

WHAT I WANT IS TO DRAW INSPIRATION
ONLY FROM THE TRUTH. . . . MY QUALIFICATIONS FOR
THIS IMPORTANT ROLE INCLUDE A LARGE HEAD,
AN ENORMOUS NOSE, DISAPPOINTMENT IN LOVE,
AND EXPECTATIONS OF ILL HEALTH.

Naguib Mahfouz

DATE: __ / __ / __

Describe your qualifications as a writer.

_____

_____

_____

_____

_____

_____

EVERYONE WANTS TO BE CARY GRANT.
EVEN I WANT TO BE CARY GRANT.

Cary Grant

DATE: __/__/__

Name the person or people you want to be.

_____

_____

_____

_____

_____

_____

DRAW A POMEGRANATE INSIDE OUT.

DRAW YOUR FAVORITE CANDY BAR INSIDE OUT.

THE WORDS
"KISS KISS BANG BANG,"
WHICH I SAW ON AN
ITALIAN MOVIE POSTER,
ARE PERHAPS THE
BRIEFEST STATEMENT
IMAGINABLE OF
THE BASIC APPEAL
OF MOVIES.

Pauline Kael

Choose four words to express the basic appeal of . . .

DATE: __/__/__

Music:

_____ _____ _____ _____

Dance:

_____ _____ _____ _____

Food:

_____ _____ _____ _____

Literature:

_____ _____ _____ _____

DATE: __/__/__

Painting:

_____ _____ _____ _____

Drama:

_____ _____ _____ _____

Architecture:

_____ _____ _____ _____

Fashion:

_____ _____ _____ _____

GRAFFITI THIS WALL.

DATE: __/__/__

DESIGN YOUR TAG.

TO TURN EVENTS INTO IDEAS IS THE FUNCTION OF LITERATURE.

George Santayana

DATE: __ / __ / __

Choose a current event. Turn it into a poem, story, or artwork here.

EUREKA! I HAVE FOUND IT!

Archimedes

DATE: __/__/__

Today's bright idea:

Doodle a roller coaster.

Doodle a Ferris wheel.

'TWAS HE THAT RANGED THE WORDS AT RANDOM FLUNG.
PIERCED THE FAIR PEARLS AND THEM TOGETHER STRUNG.

Pilpay

DATE: __/__/__

String these words together.

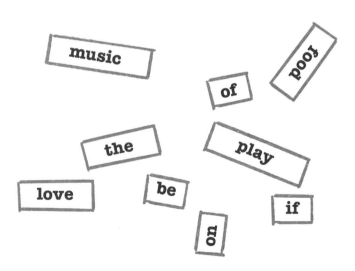

POETRY IS THE ACHIEVEMENT OF THE SYNTHESIS OF HYACINTHS AND BISCUITS.

Carl Sandburg

DATE: __/__/__

Dance is the synthesis of

_____ & _____ .

Drama is the synthesis of

_____ & _____ .

Music is the synthesis of

_____ & _____ .

Painting is the synthesis of

_____ & _____ .

Architecture is the synthesis of

_____ & _____ .

CHANGE THESE TRAFFIC SIGNS INTO POLITICAL STATEMENTS.

CHANGE THESE TRAFFIC SIGNS INTO PERSONAL STATEMENTS.

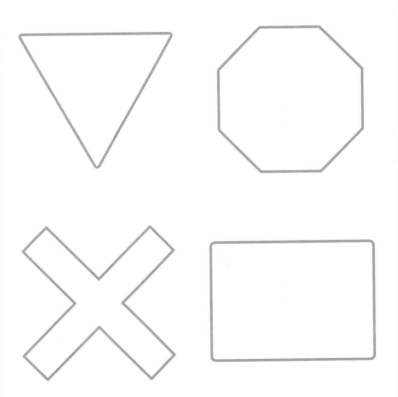

MUSIC OFT HATH SUCH A CHARM
TO MAKE BAD GOOD, AND GOOD PROVOKE TO HARM.

William Shakespeare

DATE: __/__/__

List music that inspires you to do good.

_____

_____

_____

_____

Describe what good you'll do.

_____

_____

_____

_____

IF AN IDEA'S WORTH HAVING ONCE,
IT'S WORTH HAVING TWICE.

Tom Stoppard

DATE: __/__/__

Reuse an old idea. Describe it.

_____

_____

_____

_____

_____

_____

_____

_____

_____

_____

PAINTERS AND POETS HAVE LIBERTY TO LIE.

John Ray

DATE: __/__/__

Tell a lie in a drawing.

DATE: __/__/__

Tell a lie in a rhyming couplet.

_____

_____

_____

_____

_____

_____

DATE: __/__/__

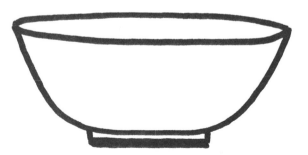

Fill the bowl with fruits in colors different from the norm.

DATE: __/__/__

Fill the vase with flowers in colors different from the norm.

DATE: __/__/__

DESCRIBE YOURSELF FROM YOUR CELL PHONE
OR TABLET'S POINT OF VIEW.

_____

_____

_____

_____

_____

_____

_____

_____

_____

DRAW YOURSELF FROM YOUR CELL PHONE'S
OR TABLET'S POINT OF VIEW.

THERE ARE ONLY TWO STYLES OF PORTRAIT PAINTING, THE SERIOUS AND THE SMIRK.

Charles Dickens

DATE: __/__/__

Draw a serious expression.

Draw a smirk.

CHARACTER IN DECAY IS THE THEME
OF THE GREAT BULK OF SUPERIOR FICTION.

H. L. Mencken

DATE: __ / __ / __

Describe a character in decay.

_____

_____

_____

_____

_____

_____

I'M INSPIRED BY...

a photograph!

DATE: __/__/__

Title:

_____

Photographer:

_____

Where I saw it:

_____

DATE: __/__/__

This photograph inspired me to:

_____

_____

_____

_____

_____

_____

THE BEST TIME FOR PLANNING A BOOK
IS WHILE YOU'RE DOING THE DISHES.

Agatha Christie

DATE: __/__/__

Do the dishes. Then write your plan for a book/story/play/poem/artwork/
design/song.

_____

_____

_____

_____

_____

_____

ALL THE REALLY GOOD IDEAS I EVER HAD CAME TO ME WHILE I WAS MILKING A COW.

Grant Wood

DATE: __ / __ / __

Milk a cow (or drink a glass of milk). Then write your good ideas.

_____

_____

_____

_____

_____

_____

_____

WHAT IS THE SPHINX THINKING?

WHAT IS THE THINKER THINKING?

IT ISN'T SO MUCH WHAT'S ON THE TABLE THAT MATTERS, AS WHAT'S ON THE CHAIRS.

Sir William Schwenck

DATE: __/__/__

Fill out the seating plan at your table for a dinner party of writers.

Fill out the seating plan at your table for a dinner party of actors.

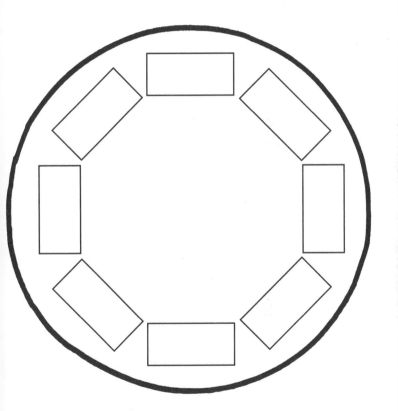

I DREAM FOR A LIVING.

Steven Spielberg

DATE: __/__/__

Describe your most recent daydream.

_____

_____

_____

_____

_____

_____

_____

_____

I SUPPOSE I HAVE A HIGHLY DEVELOPED CAPACITY
FOR SELF-DELUSION, SO IT'S NO PROBLEM FOR ME
TO BELIEVE I AM SOMEBODY ELSE.

Daniel Day-Lewis

DATE: __ /__ /__

Describe who you believe you are.

_____

_____

_____

_____

_____

_____

_____

FIRST THOUGHT, BEST THOUGHT.

Jack Kerouac

DATE: __/__/__

Quick! Write something.

_____

_____

_____

_____

_____

_____

_____

JUST DASH SOMETHING DOWN IF YOU SEE A BLANK
CANVAS STARING AT YOU WITH A CERTAIN IMBECILITY.

Vincent van Gogh

DATE: _/_/_

Quick! Draw something.

A RHYMER AND A POET ARE TWO THINGS.

Ben Jonson

DATE: __/__/__

Create a love poem from the rhyme "Roses are red, violets are blue. Sugar is sweet, and so are you."

_____

_____

_____

_____

_____

_____

DATE: __/__/__

Make a match.

_____

+

_____

DATE: __ / __ / __

Create a menu for a romantic story.

_____

_____

_____

_____

_____

_____

DATE: __ / __ / __

Create a menu for an adventure story.

_____

_____

_____

_____

_____

_____

Do I love cooking?
Yeah, I do.
But that's not why
I do this. I do this
because food is
a great vehicle for
entertainment,
a viable subject
for storytelling.

Alton Brown

doo

Doodle heaven.

Doodle hell.

THE COVERS OF THIS BOOK ARE TOO FAR APART.

Ambrose Bierce

DATE: __/__/__

Write a scathing one-sentence book review.

_____

_____

_____

_____

_____

_____

DATE: __/__/__

Write a raving one-sentence book review.

_____

_____

_____

_____

_____

_____

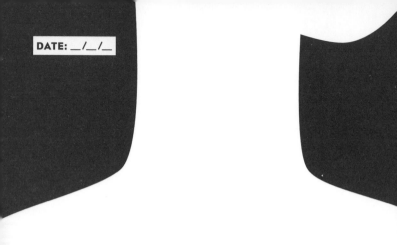

DATE: __/__/__

DESIGN A NECKLACE FROM ITEMS YOU FIND IN YOUR TOOLBOX.

DATE: _/_/_

DESIGN A BELT FROM ITEMS YOU FIND IN YOUR JEWELRY BOX.

HARD FEATURES EVERY BUNGLER CAN COMMAND;
TO DRAW TRUE BEAUTY SHOWS A MASTER'S HAND.

John Dryden

DATE: __/__/__

Are you a bungler or a master? Draw a beautiful or ugly nose.

THINGS THAT GAIN BY BEING PAINTED:
PINES. AUTUMN FIELDS. MOUNTAIN VILLAGES AND PATHS.
CRANES AND DEER. A VERY COLD WINTER SCENE;
AN UNSPEAKABLY HOT SUMMER SCENE.

Sei Shōnagon

DATE: __ /__ /__

Pick one of these and paint it here.

Then learnedst thou
how much harder
it is to give properly
than to take
properly, and that
bestowing well
is an art—the last,
subtlest master art
of kindness.

Friedrich Wilhelm Nietzsche

DATE: __/__/__

Most thoughtful gifts you have given:

_____

_____

_____

_____

_____

_____

DATE: __/__/__

Most thoughtful gifts you have received:

_____

_____

_____

_____

_____

_____

ALL I NEED TO MAKE A COMEDY IS A PARK, A POLICEMAN, AND A PRETTY GIRL.

Charlie Chaplin

DATE: __/__/__

Describe what happens in this comedy.

_____

_____

_____

_____

_____

_____

DATE: __/__/__

Describe what happens in a tragedy with the same three elements.

_____

_____

_____

_____

_____

_____

DESIGN A COIN.

FRONT

BACK

DESIGN A BILL.

FRONT

BACK

A MERE COPIER OF NATURE
CAN NEVER PRODUCE ANYTHING GREAT.

Sir Joshua Reynolds

DATE: __/__/__

Draw a leaf with personality.

LITERATURE IS FULL OF PERFUMES.

Walt Whitman

DATE: __ / __ / __

Describe a scene from a book in fragrances.

_____

_____

_____

_____

_____

_____

_____

I'M INSPIRED BY...
a work of literature!

DATE: __/__/__

Title:

_____

Author:

_____

Genre:

_____

DATE: __/__/__

Reading this inspired me to:

_____

_____

_____

_____

_____

_____

MAKE A COMB HARMONICA:
CUT WAXED PAPER THE LENGTH OF A COMB AND TWICE ITS WIDTH.
FOLD THE PAPER OVER THE TEETH OF THE COMB.
HOLD THE COMB FIRMLY WITH THE TEETH UPWARD
AND HUM THROUGH THE PAPER.

List the tunes you can play.

_____

_____

_____

_____

_____

_____

LISTEN FOR A BIRD SONG. WRITE DOWN THE SOUNDS
THAT MOST CLOSELY MATCH THE SONG.

ONE LINE HAS NO MEANING; A SECOND LINE IS NEEDED TO GIVE IT EXPRESSION.

Eugène Delacroix

DATE: __/__/__

Give expression to this line.

DATE: __/__/__

Give expression to this line.

A GUILTY CONSCIENCE NEEDS TO CONFESS.
A WORK OF ART IS A CONFESSION.

Albert Camus

DATE: __/__/__

Make a confession in words or art.

I HATE WRITING,
BUT I LOVE HAVING WRITTEN.

Robert Louis Stevenson

DATE: __/__/__

I hate

_____

_____ ,

but I love having

_____

_____ .

MOST OF THE
BASIC MATERIAL
A WRITER
WORKS WITH
IS ACQUIRED
BEFORE THE AGE
OF FIFTEEN.

Willa Cather

DATE: __/__/__

Record your "material" from ages zero to seven.

_____

_____

_____

_____

_____

_____

DATE: __/__/__

Record your "material" from ages eight to fifteen.

_____

_____

_____

_____

_____

_____

WE LOOK TOO MUCH TO MUSEUMS.
THE SUN COMING UP IN THE MORNING IS ENOUGH.

Ralph Ellison

DATE: __ / __ / __

Describe what is enough for you.

_____

_____

_____

_____

_____

_____

POP ART IS ABOUT LIKING THINGS.

Andy Warhol

DATE: __/__/__

Draw a product you like in its package.

CREATE A TITLE FOR A MYSTERY NOVEL.

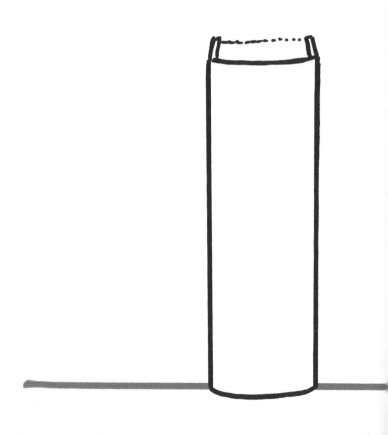

DESIGN THE COVER OF THE BOOK.

DATE: __/__/__

Cross out the "wrong" words in this passage from *Tom Sawyer*.
(Answer on bottom of page.)

About midnight, under an inky sky, Tom arrived with a freshly boiled ham and a few tasty trifles, and stopped at last in a dense undergrowth on a small, rocky bluff over-looking the set meeting place.

DATE: __/__/__

Cross out the "wrong" words in this passage from *Pride and Prejudice*.
(Answer on bottom of page.)

Elizabeth awoke and arose early the next
morning to the same disturbing thoughts and
troubling meditations, which had finally at
length closed her sad, weary eyes the night
before.

Doodle noise.

Doodle silence.

DATE: __/__/__

Embellish the alphabet.

A B C D E

F G H I J K

L M N O P

Q R S T U

V W X Y Z

DATE: __/__/__

Add an illuminated letter to this medieval manuscript.

LIE ON YOUR BACK OUTDOORS
AND DRAW WHAT YOU SEE.

GO TO THE TOP OF A BUILDING
AND DRAW WHAT YOU SEE LOOKING DOWN.

You don't have to suffer to be a poet. Adolescence is enough suffering for anyone.

John Ciardi

DATE: __/__/__

Describe a painful moment from adolescence.

_____

_____

_____

_____

_____

_____

DATE: __/__/__

Transform your adolescent experience into an art form.

DATE: __/__/__

Design the furniture arrangement for a chatty living room.

DATE: __/__/__

Fill the seats of this living room with chatty guests you know or wish you knew.

I LIKE ALL THE CHAIRS
TO TALK TO
ONE ANOTHER AND
TO THE SOFAS
AND NOT THOSE
PARLOR-CAR
ARRANGEMENTS THAT
CREATE TWO SIBERIAS.

Mario Buatta

THE TWO
MOST ENGAGING
POWERS OF
AN AUTHOR:
NEW THINGS ARE
MADE FAMILIAR,
AND
FAMILIAR THINGS
ARE MADE NEW.

Samuel Johnson

DATE: __ / __ / __

Describe a brand new electronic device in a way that your grandmother
would understand.

_____

_____

_____

_____

_____

_____

DATE: __ / __ / __

Describe a new use for an umbrella in a way that would excite a
bored teenager.

_____

_____

_____

_____

_____

> ## ABOUT HALF MY DESIGNS ARE ARE TOTAL MADNESS, AND THE DESIGNS. ▶ *Manolo Blahnik*

DATE: __/__/__

Draw three shoes, one of each type.

TOTAL MADNESS

CONTROLLED FANTASY

BREAD-AND-BUTTER

CONTROLLED FANTASY, 15 PERCENT REST ARE BREAD-AND-BUTTER

DATE: __/__/__

Draw three hats, one of each type.

TOTAL MADNESS

CONTROLLED FANTASY

BREAD-AND-BUTTER

DESIGN IS
NOT JUST WHAT
IT LOOKS LIKE
AND FEELS LIKE.
DESIGN IS
HOW IT WORKS.

Steve Jobs

DATE: __/__/__

List products that look beautiful and work well.

_____

_____

_____

_____

_____

_____

DATE: __/__/__

List products that look beautiful but don't work well.

_____

_____

_____

_____

_____

_____

DATE: __/__/__

REDUCE THE 272 WORDS OF THE GETTYSBURG ADDRESS

TO A 140-CHARACTER TWEET.

Fourscore and seven years ago our fathers brought forth, on this continent, a new nation, conceived in liberty, and dedicated to the proposition that all men are created equal. Now we are engaged in a great civil war, testing whether that nation, or any nation so conceived, and so dedicated, can long endure. We are met on a great battle-field of that war. We have come to dedicate a portion of that field, as a final resting-place for those who here gave their lives, that that nation might live. It is altogether fitting and proper that we should do this. But, in a larger sense, we cannot dedicate, we cannot consecrate—we cannot hallow—this ground. The brave men, living and dead, who struggled here, have consecrated it far above our poor power to add or detract. The world will little note, nor long remember what we say here, but it can never forget what they did here. It is for us the living, rather, to be dedicated here to the unfinished work which they who fought here have thus far so nobly advanced. It is rather for us to be here dedicated to the great task remaining before us—that from these honored dead we take increased devotion to that cause for which they here gave the last full measure of devotion—that we here highly resolve that these dead shall not have died in vain—that this nation, under God, shall have a new birth of freedom, and that government of the people, by the people, for the people, shall not perish from the earth.

REDUCE EDVARD MUNCH'S *THE SCREAM* TO AN EMOTICON.

I'M INSPIRED BY...

a work of art!

DATE: _ / _ / _

Title:

_____

Artist:

_____

Style:

_____

Medium:

_____

Where I saw it:

_____

DATE: _ / _ / _

This artwork inspired me to:

_____

_____

_____

Create a design on a sweatshirt that commemorates an experience.

Look at the clouds in the sky. Draw one pattern you see there.

ART IS THE IMPOSING OF PATTERN ON EXPERIENCE, AND OUR AESTHETIC ENJOYMENT IS RECOGNITION OF THE PATTERN.

Alfred North Whitehead

IF YOU CAN WALK, YOU CAN DANCE.

Zimbabwean saying

DATE: __ /__ /__

List forms of creativity that come to you as easily as walking.

_____

_____

_____

_____

_____

_____

_____

IT HAS TAKEN ME YEARS OF STRUGGLE, HARD WORK, AND RESEARCH TO LEARN TO MAKE ONE SIMPLE GESTURE.

Isadora Duncan

DATE: __/__/__

List forms of creativity that require struggle, hard work, and research for you.

_____

_____

_____

_____

_____

_____

_____

IN THE FACTORY, WE MAKE COSMETICS;

DATE: __/__/__

Use colored pencils or paints to make up this face for the red carpet.

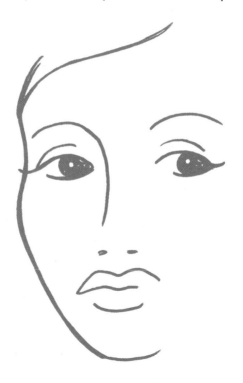

DATE: __/__/__

Use colored pencils or paints to make up this face for a job interview.

COME UP WITH AN ACTIVITY OF YOUR OWN THAT INSPIRES
CREATIVITY. POST YOUR IDEA AND YOUR RESULTS WITH
#DOONETHINGEVERYDAYTHATINSPIRESYOU.

DATE: __/__/__

ACKNOWLEDGMENTS

I would like to thank the following friends, family members, teachers, colleagues, and random strangers for sparking, nurturing, encouraging, or enduring my most inspired year:

_____ for: _____

_____ for: _____

_____ for: _____

_____ for: _____

_____ for: _____

_____ for: _____

DATE: __/__/__

ABOUT THE AUTHOR

Write your biography, flaunting your creativity.

_____

_____

_____

_____

_____

_____

_____

_____

_____

_____

_____

_____

_____

Draw or paste in your author portrait here.

POTTER STYLE

Copyright © 2015 by ROBIE LLC. All rights reserved.
Published in the United States by Potter Style, an imprint of the
Crown Publishing Group, a division of Penguin Random House LLC, New York.

www.crownpublishing.com
www.potterstyle.com

POTTER STYLE and colophon are registered trademarks
of Penguin Random House LLC.

Library of Congress Cataloging-in-Publication Data
Smith, Dian G.
Do one thing every day that inspires you : a portfolio of creativity /
Dian G. Smith and Robie Rogge. — First edition.
pages cm
1. Creative ability. 2. Diaries—Authorship. I. Rogge, Robie. II. Title.
BF408.S494 2015
153.3'5—dc23
2014047659

ISBN 978-0-553-44788-0

Printed in China

CONCEIVED AND COMPILED BY Robie Rogge and Dian G. Smith
COVER DESIGN BY Danielle Deschenes
INTERIOR DESIGN & ILLUSTRATIONS BY Rae Ann Spitzenberger & woolypear

10 9 8 7 6 5 4 3 2

First Edition